顛倒看世界

我是誰？

文·圖　MARUTAN
譯　謝依玲

你看到的是什麼？看事情的方法不只一種喔！

What do you see? There is more than one way.

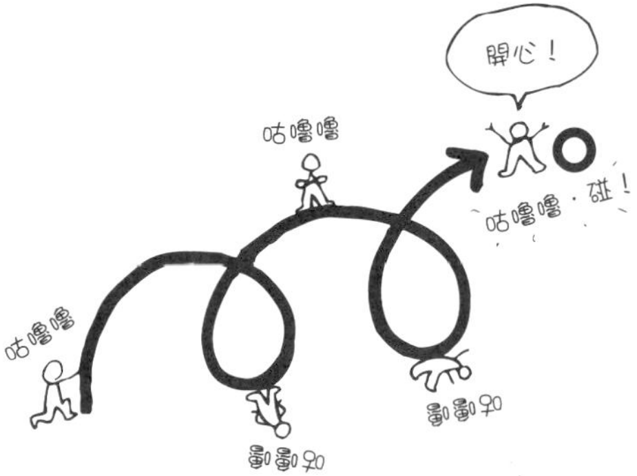

嗨！很高興認識你！在自我介紹之前，
先讓我們上下顛倒一下吧！
試試看！看到什麼了嗎？我們看起來完全不一樣了對吧！
「咕嚕嚕」的轉個圈，就可以「碰！」的一下，變身！
「咕嚕嚕」的顛倒過來看世界，就會「碰！」的一下，變快樂！
失敗或是想哭的時候，
跟我們玩一下「咕嚕嚕・碰！」，就會覺得——沒什麼大不了的嘛！
吵架的時候也「咕嚕嚕・碰！」一下，——跟他和好吧！
帶點不可思議的驚喜，給你快樂心情的好朋友，
我們就是「咕嚕嚕・碰！」

Before you ask about us, please turn us upside down!
Try it! What do you see? We look totally different, don't we?
We turn into something else when you change the way you look at us.
When you are sad or feel like crying,
if you have been told off by Mom or you don't like your friends
because you've been fighting....Play with us! We're sure you'll feel so much better.
You'll like your friends again by changing the way you look at them,
like when you see the other side of us! We are fun and mysterious and are your best friends,
cheering you up anywhere, anytime. We're called KURURINPA!

在冰山上搖搖晃晃的走路。我是誰？

I like to play on the icebergs. Who am I ?

噠噠噠噠，

我是牧場上的賽跑冠軍。我是誰？

I can win a running race! Who am I ?

汪汪！一起去散步吧！我是誰？

Let's go for a walk. Who am I ?

呼嚕呼嚕，我是森林裡的博士。我是誰？

I am the wisest in the forest. Who am I ?

嗯～我最喜歡吃蜂蜜！我是誰？

I love honey! Who am I ?

吱吱吱，我最愛吃香蕉。我是誰？

I love bananas! Who am I ?

咕嚕咕嚕，
用鼻子把球頂起來轉一轉。我是誰？
I can balance a ball very well! Who am I ?

左蹦蹦，右跳跳。我是誰？
I play hop skip and jump. Who am I ?

喵——喵，老鼠別跑！我是誰？

I love to chase after mice! Who am I ?

我們有長長的脖子，
可以看到很～遠的地方。我們是誰？

We can see far away with our long necks. Who are we ?

嚎——

我可以用長鼻子做很多事。我是誰？

I can do many things with my long nose. Who am I ?

我優雅的在水上滑行。我是誰？

I am a graceful swimmer. Who am I ?

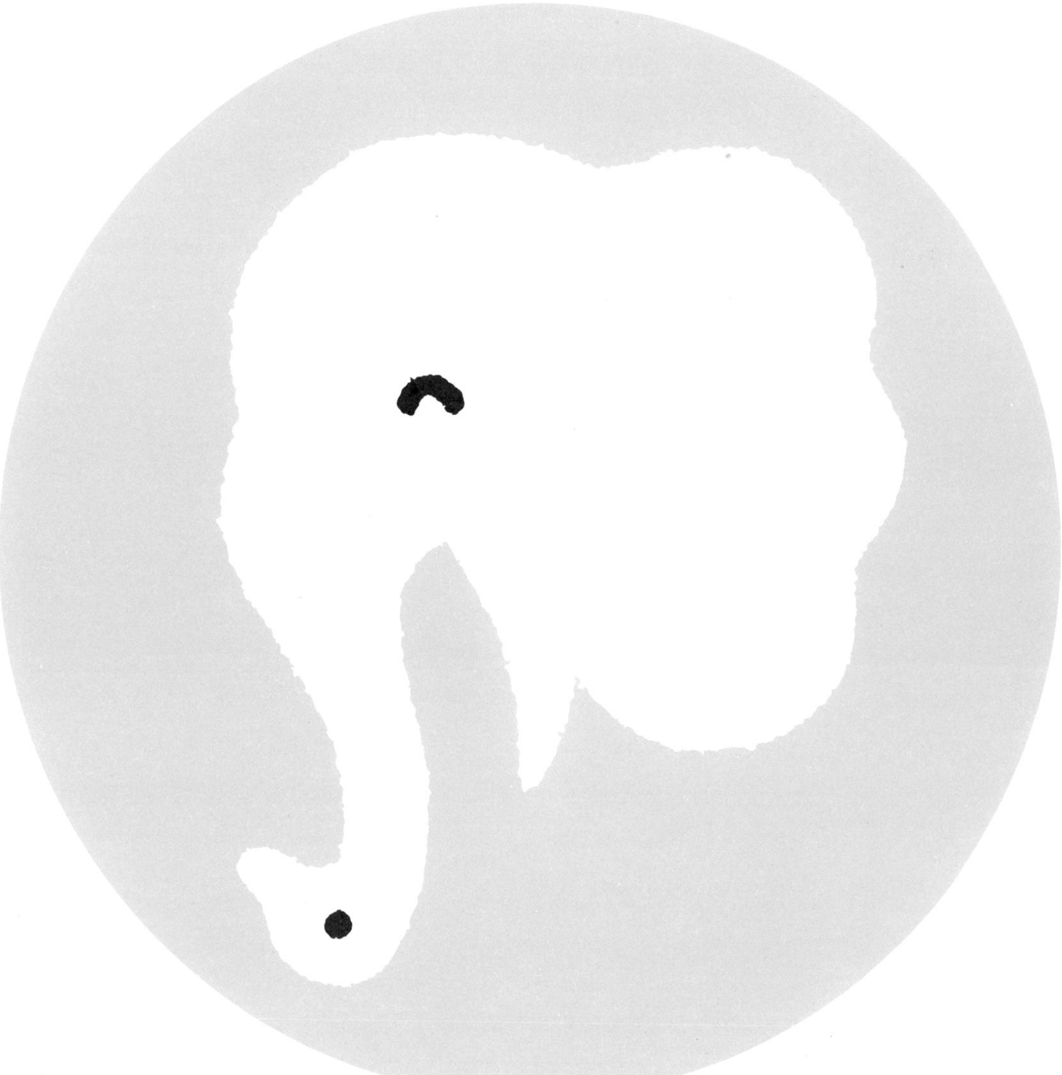

呼嚕呼嚕，在樹上打瞌睡。我是誰？

I nap in the trees. Who am I ?

我有長耳朵，
總是蹦蹦跳跳。我是誰？

I have long ears. Who am I ?

喀哩喀哩，我最喜歡吃松果！我是誰？

I love nuts. Who am I ?

我有黃色和黑色的斑紋。我是誰？

I wear yellow and black fur. Who am I ?

我最喜歡在河裡洗澡。我是誰？

I love to bath. Who am I ?

在有月亮的晚上悄悄出沒。我是誰？

I enjoy a night out. Who am I ?

我有好多腳，都要纏在一起啦！我是誰？

I have many long arms and legs! Who am I ?

叮叮噹，叮叮噹，

聖誕夜最忙碌了。我是誰？

I am busy on Christmas Eve. Who am I ?

噗——噗——我的肚子又餓啦！我是誰？

I am always hungry! Who am I ?

我把房子背在背上走。我是誰？

I carry my house on my back. Who am I ?

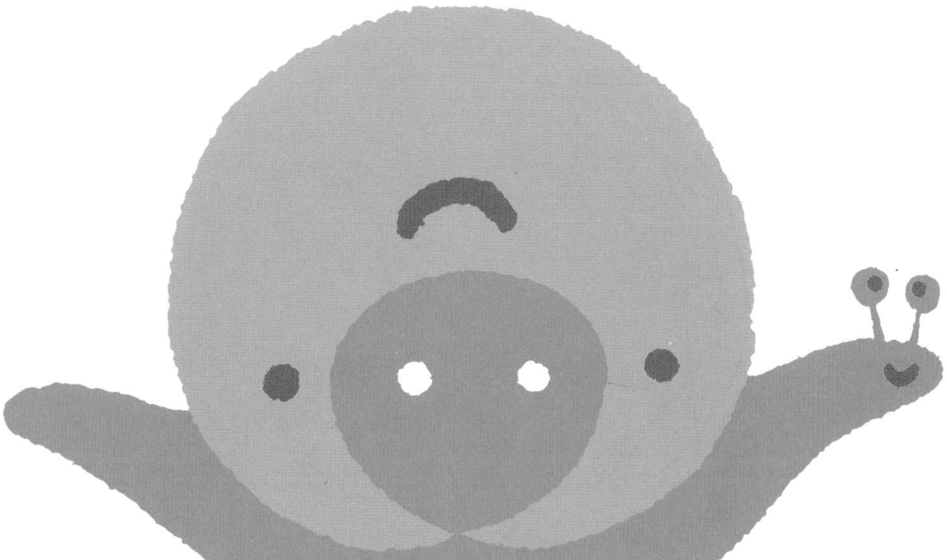

我的背上有許多黑點點。我是誰？

I have pretty dots on my back. Who am I ?

吼——

我是最勇猛的萬獸之王！我是誰？

I am the king of the beasts! Who am I ?

嘓！嘓！我一跳就可以跳很遠。我是誰？

I can leap very far. Who am I ?

哞——哞——

我常常在草原上閒晃。我是誰？

I love to lounge in the meadow. Who am I ?

我穿著厚厚的黑白大衣。我是誰？

I wear a warm, black and white coat. Who am I ?

我是翩翩起舞的花間仙子。我是誰？

I am a dancer on the flowers. Who am I ?

大大的嘴巴裡有一排長長的牙齒，我是誰？

I have a huge mouth with many teeth. Who am I ?

長長的身體，嘶嘶嘶的往前爬，
其實我沒那麼可怕啦！我是誰？

People think I am scary, but I am not. Who am I ?

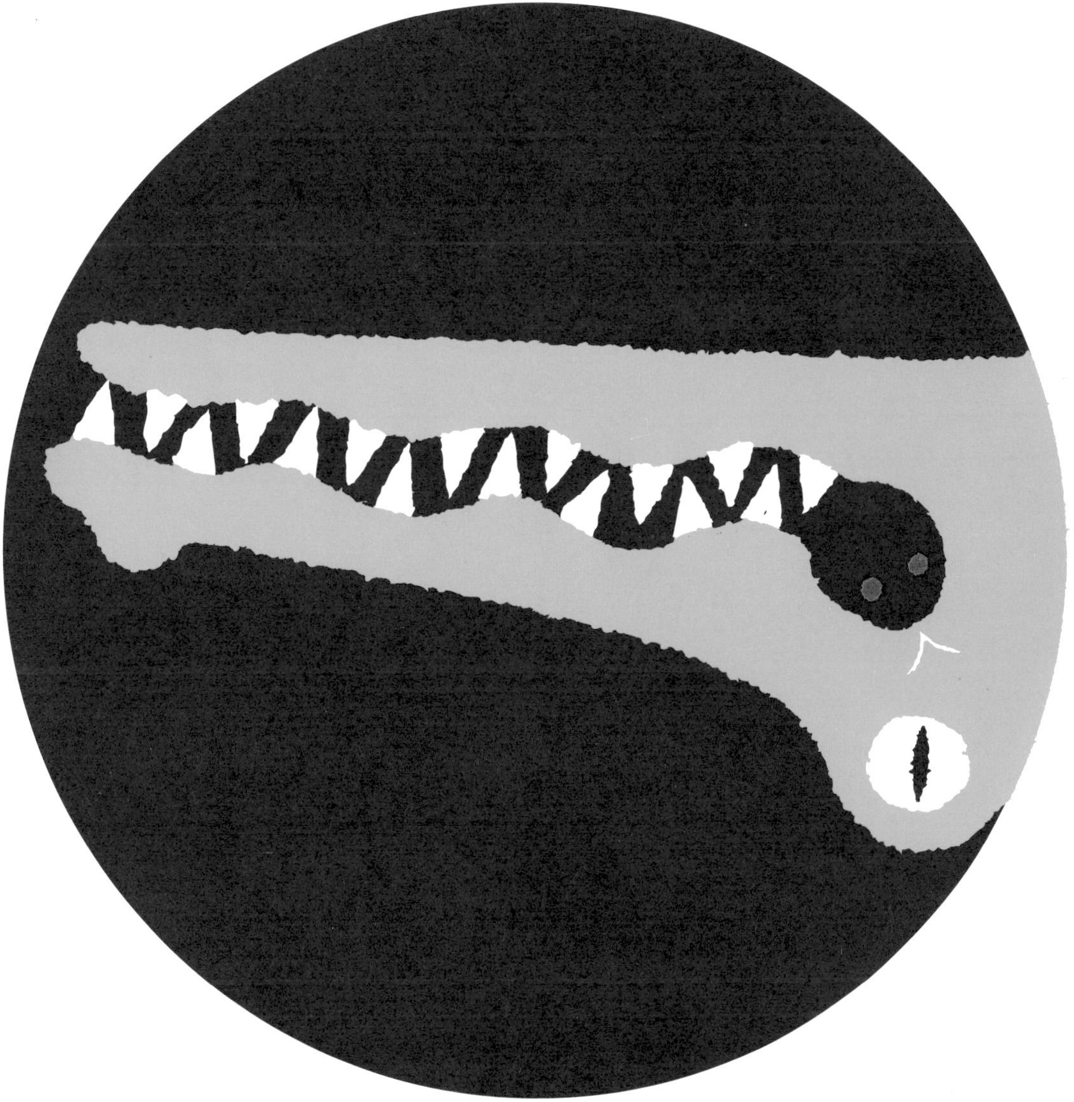

顛倒看世界

我是誰？

文．圖　MARUTAN
譯　謝依玲

請把這本書顛倒過來，再讀一遍吧！

作者簡介

MARUTAN

後藤徹、後藤靜子夫妻組成的創作團體。

後藤徹，1951年生於東京，東京藝術大學版畫研究所畢業，現為廣告創意總監，作品曾獲得包括紐約ADC賞在內的多項大獎。後藤靜子，1953年生於東京，東京造型大學室內建築科畢業，現為室內設計師。夫婦兩人合力創作的顛倒書「咕嚕嚕．碰！」系列（KURURINPA），希望告訴孩子們「看事情的方法不只一種」。2004年參與日本UNESCO（聯合國教科文組織）促進協會的「世界寺子屋運動」以來，在越南、印度、加拿大、美國也陸續舉辦相關畫展與創作工坊。

譯者簡介

謝依玲

「咕嚕嚕．碰！」把名字顛倒過來念，就變成「〇一蟹」，是種不安於淡水也不安於海水，喜歡到處跑的螃蟹。臺灣大學化學研究所畢業，在誠品書店兒童館發現新世界之後，現於日本專攻兒童文學與繪本研究。譯有本書的姊妹作《顛倒看世界：我是什麼？》。

小魯寶寶書 12 顛倒看世界 我是誰？

文．圖／MARUTAN　譯／謝依玲

發行人／陳衛平

出版者／小魯文化事業股份有限公司

地址／106 臺北市安居街六號十二樓

電話／(02)27320708　傳真／(02)27327455

E-mail／service@tienwei.com.tw

網址／www.tienwei.com.tw

出版總監／沙永玲　副總編輯／鄭如瑤

執行編輯／周佩穎　美術編輯／張雅玫

郵政劃撥／18696791帳號

出版登記證／局版北市業字第543號

初版／西元2007年8月

初版四刷／西元2008年7月

定價／新臺幣230元

ISBN／978-986-211-001-0